Configuration Management

IT Infrastructure Library

LONDON: THE STATIONERY OFFICE

CCTA

Central Computer and Telecommunications Agency

Published by permission of Stichting EXIN
under licence from the Controller of HMSO

Applications for reproduction should be made to
Her Majesty's Stationery Office, The Copyright
Unit, St Clements House, 2-16 Colegate
Norwich NR3 1BQ

ISBN 0 11 330530 3
ISSN 0956 2591

This is one of the books published in the IT
Infrastructure Library series.

For further information on CCTA products,
contact:

CCTA Library,
Rosebery Court,
St Andrews Court
NORWICH NR7 0HS.
Telephone 01603 704930
GTN 3040 4930

This document has been produced using
procedures conforming to
BSI 5750 Part 1: 1987; ISO 9001:1987.

Table of contents

Foreword

Welcome to the IT Infrastructure Library **Configuration Management** *module.*

In their respective subject areas, the IT Infrastructure Library publications complement and provide more detail than the IS Guides.

The ethos behind the development of the IT Infrastructure Library is the recognition that organizations are becoming increasingly dependent on IT in order to satisfy their corporate aims and meet their business needs. This growing dependency leads to a growing requirement for high-quality IT services. In this context quality means matched to business needs and user requirements as these evolve.

This module is one of a series of codes of practice intended to facilitate the quality management of IT Services, and of the IT Infrastructure. (By IT Infrastructure, we mean organizations' computers and networks - hardware, software and computer-related telecommunications, upon which applications systems and IT services are built and run). The codes of practice are intended to assist organizations to provide quality IT service in the face of skill shortages, system complexity, rapid change, current and future user requirements, growing user expectations, etc.

Underpinning the IT Infrastructure is the Environmental Infrastructure upon which it is built. Environmental topics are covered in a separate set of guides within the IT Infrastructure Library.

IT Infrastructure Management is a complex subject which for presentational and practical reasons has been broken down within the IT Infrastructure Library into a series of modules. A complete list of current and planned modules is available from the CCTA IT Infrastructure Management Services at the address given at the back of this module.

The structure of this module is in essence :

* *a Management Summary aimed at senior managers (Directors of IT and above, senior IT people and in some cases "senior customers" (typically Civil Service grades 3 - 7)*

* *the main body of the text aimed at IT middle management (typically grades 7 to HEO)*

* *technical detail in Annexes.*

*The module gives the main **guidance** in Sections 3 to 5; explains the **benefits, costs and possible problems** in Section 6, which may be of interest to senior staff; and provides information on **tools** (requirements and examples of real-life availability) in Section 7.*

CCTA is working with the IT industry to foster the development of software tools to underpin the guidance contained within the codes of practice (ie to make adherence to the module more practicable), and ultimately to automate functions.

If you have any comments on this or other modules, do please let us know. A comment sheet is provided with every module; please feel free to photocopy the comment sheet or to let us have your views via any other medium.

Thank you. We hope you find this module useful.

1. Management summary

Introduction

No organization can be fully efficient or effective unless it manages its assets, particularly if the assets are vital to the running of the organizations' business. Organizations are becoming increasingly dependent on their IT assets. Their businesses require quality IT services, and cost pressures mean that services must be provided economically. Configuration management provides IT management with direct control over the IT assets of the organization and helps organizations deliver quality IT service economically.

A description

Configuration management is a discipline, normally supported by software tools, that gives IT management precise control over IT assets by allowing IT management to:

* specify the versions of configuration items (CIs) in use and in existence on an IT infrastructure and information on

  - the status of these items (eg in live use, archived, scheduled for live use)

  - who owns each item (the individual with prime responsibility for it)

  - the relationships between items

* maintain up to date records containing these pieces of information

* control changes to the CIs by ensuring changes are made only with the agreement of appropriate named authorities

* audit the IT infrastructure to ensure it contains the authorized CIs and only these CIs.

The items that may be brought under configuration management control include hardware devices, computer programs, documentation, telecommunication services, computer centre facilities and any others that the organization wishes to control.

Benefits

Configuration management contributes to the economic provision of quality IT services:

* by making cheaper and less error prone the management of changes and upgrades to the IT infrastructure (the make up of changes can be defined precisely, eg as package releases, for management authorization; and configuration management can help identify CIs that might be affected by changes to other CIs)

* by making it easier to handle IT service problems (configuration management can help to identify CIs that may be affected by problems in related CIs)

* by simplifying the task of user support via the Help Desk (the Help Desk can easily check which items the user is using or connected to, whether items in use are as authorized, whether the items have been affected by changes/problems, which other related items may be at the root cause of any problems).

Configuration management also makes it more difficult for malicious changes to be made to the IT infrastructure and therefore improves security.

Configuration management provides a definitive check that items reported to the Help Desk or found during configuration audits are legally owned.

Using configuration management data, management information can be gathered (eg trends in problems affecting particular CI types from particular suppliers or development groups) for later proactive use in improving the quality and/or economy of IT service provision.

For further information on the benefits of configuration management please see section 6.

Automated support

As IT systems become larger, more complex and subject to frequent change, configuration management, though more difficult, becomes more important.

Many organizations already have some form of configuration management in operation, often paper based. For today's large and complex IT infrastructures, configuration management will operate more effectively when supported by a software tool that is capable of maintaining a Configuration Management Database (CMDB). The CMDB contains details about the attributes and the history of each CI and details of the important relationships between CIs.

This module

This module provides guidance on all aspects of configuration management including planning, implementing and running a configuration management function to control the components of 'live' systems; and also outlines the interfaces required to configuration management systems for applications development projects.

The module gives guidance on the facilities required of configuration management support tools.

The module concentrates on the control of hardware, software, and documentation held in electronic form.

The module also describes methods for auditing the configuration management function to ensure conformance with the guidance provided in this module, and gives metrics for measuring the effectiveness and efficiency of the configuration management group.

Finally...

Because configuration management leads to improved IT service provision at lower cost, all organizations should consider implementing a configuration management system as early as possible.

2. Introduction

Configuration management is a discipline which can be used for controlling all components of an IT infrastructure. In configuration management terminology, IT infrastructure components are called Configuration Items (CIs). CIs include hardware items, software components, network items, documentation and any part of the IT infrastructure or items associated with it which the organization wishes to control.

An important part of configuration management is deciding the level at which control is to be exercised - with top level CIs broken down into components which are themselves CIs, and so on. To provide an illustration, figure 1 shows System A - which consists of components A1, A2, A3, and A4. Each of these components can be broken down into smaller components. In this example A3 is made up of A3.1, A3.2 and A3.3. Each of the components shown are configuration items (CIs), including the total system.

Figure 1: Configuration breakdown

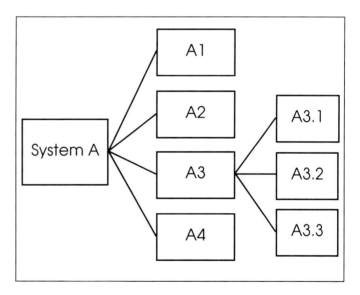

System A can be said to be the 'parent CI' of component A3. The sub-component A3.1 can be identified as a 'child CI' of component A3.

Normally CIs are defined down to the lowest level at which a component can be independently installed, replaced or modified. For example it would not be worth identifying software modules individually if the lowest level at which changes can be made is the complete software program. At various times, depending on who wants to use the information and for what purposes, the level at which CI information needs to be defined or extracted may change.

2.1 Purpose

The main purpose of this module is to give guidance on the planning and operation of IT infrastructure configuration management. The module outlines how configuration management can help IT management more effectively to control hardware and software assets, manage changes, handle incidents and problems and in general provide users with a quality IT service economically.

2.2 Target readership

This module is aimed IT services managers, staff who are or will be responsible for configuration management, change managers, help desk staff, computer operations managers, network managers, problem managers, staff responsible for testing and acceptance of new IT components (hardware and software) and staff responsible for the control and distribution of software. It may also be of interest to applications development managers and senior user managers.

2.3 Scope

Configuration management, as applied to IT infrastructure management, consists of four basic functions:

* **identification** - specifying and identifying all components of an IT infrastructure

* **control** - the ability to agree and 'freeze' CIs and then to make changes only with the agreement of appropriate named authorities

* **status accounting** - the recording and reporting of all current and historical data concerned with each CI

* **verification** - a series of reviews and audits to ensure that there is conformity between all CIs and the authorized state of CIs as recorded in the configuration management database (CMDB).

In the example shown at figure 1, identification is concerned with naming and listing the CIs shown and describing the relationships between them.

Control is concerned with ensuring that none of the CIs shown is altered or replaced, and that no CIs are added, without appropriate authorization.

Status accounting maintains records of the current, previous and planned states and attributes of the CIs and tracks these states and attributes: for example, as the status of a CI changes from 'development' through to 'test', 'scheduled to go live', 'live', and through to 'archived'.

Verification is concerned with checking that the physical CIs actually match the authorized system as described in the CMDB.

The procedures needed for **identification, status accounting** and **verification** are described in sections 3.1, 4.1 and 5.1 of this module.

Some of the procedures needed for configuration **control** are touched upon in this module which covers in general terms the control of change associated with software releases and hardware installation (especially in relation to maintaining the CMDB up to date), but more detailed guidance is available in the following modules. Change control and authorization procedures are detailed in the **Change Management** module. The procedures required for the control of software are described in the **Software Control & Distribution** module. The physical control of hardware is covered in the **Computer Installation & Acceptance** module, whilst the **Management of Local Processors & Terminals** module covers the installation and control of terminals and small computers.

Many organizations are already using some elements of configuration management, often with paper based systems. In practical terms for today's large and complex IT infrastructures, configuration management requires the use of a support tool which includes a configuration management database (CMDB). The CMDB is likely to be based upon relational database technology, which provides for very flexible and powerful interrogation facilities. A few examples of potential use are:

* to list all the component CIs and their version numbers, within a packaged release

* to identify the CIs affected by a scheduled (authorized) change

* to list all requests for change (RFCs) relating to one particular CI

* to identify all CIs purchased from a particular supplier within a specific period

* to identify all equipment at a given location, for example to assist in an audit.

Configuration management can be used to manage the components of any system or project. It could, for instance, be applied to the building of a battleship, or to its components and equipment once it has been built. This module deals primarily with configuration management as it applies to the ongoing management and control of 'live' IT systems. CCTA recommends that a single configuration management system should be used which also controls components of IT systems during development projects. Although applications development is outside the scope of this module, the module describes how CIs should be transferred from the development to the live environments when such a common configuration management system is in use. Fuller information about the use of configuration management for development projects can be found in the CCTA **PRINCE Configuration Management Guide**, which is part of the PRINCE documentation.

2.4 Related guidance

This book is one of a series of modules issued as part of the CCTA IT Infrastructure Library. Although this module can be read in isolation, it should be used in conjunction with other IT Infrastructure modules.

The **Change Management** module describes procedures for authorizing and implementing IT infrastructure changes. Ideally change management should be regarded as an integral part of a configuration management system. However, because many installations have been practising change management without adopting full configuration management, the subject is treated separately.

Configuration management contributes to the effective control of incidents and problems. Information on this is available in the **Problem Management** and **Help Desk** modules.

The process of physically controlling software can be regarded as part of configuration management. The **Software Control and Distribution** (SC&D) module covers the building, distribution and implementation of software package releases in detail. The Configuration Management module covers in general terms the procedures required for the control of software package releases, but concentrates on the actions needed to maintain an up-to-date logical model of the IT infrastructure. This logical model is used to control and record the details of the building, release, distribution, implementation and maintenance of software releases.

Configuration management is used to control the movement of components into and out of independent testing environments. The **Testing Software for Operational Use** module covers this topic.

All items to be presented for acceptance into the live environment must be registered in the configuration management system and brought under configuration management control. The SC&D module covers this for software. The module on **Computer Installation and Acceptance** covers the actions required for hardware items and the **Network Management** module does the same for communications equipment. The module on the **Management of Local Processors & Terminals** covers the actions required for terminals and small computers.

2.5 Standards

CCTA SSADM and PRINCE

CCTA recommends that a single configuration management system is used to control components in both live and development environments. SSADM is the recommended standard systems analysis and design method used in Government whilst PRINCE is the recommended standard project management method.

ISO9001/EN29000/BS5750 - Quality Management and Quality Assurance Standards

The IT Infrastructure Library modules are being designed to assist adherents to obtain third-party quality certification to ISO9001. Organizations' IT Directorates may wish to be so certified and CCTA will in future recommend that Facilities Management providers are also certified, by a third-party certification body, to ISO9000. Such third-parties should be accredited by the NACCB, the National Accreditation Council for Certification Bodies.

BS6488 - Code of Practice for Configuration Management of Computer-based systems (1984)

The guidance in this module adheres to the code of practice embodied in BS6488 but expands and gives more detail for configuration management of IT infrastructures.

3. Planning for configuration management

This section describes the planning that is required once a decision has been taken to adopt configuration management.

The planning and implementation activities described in sections 3 and 4 should be regarded as a project and controlled using a recognized project management method such as PRINCE.

The IT Services Manager must appoint a Configuration Manager, whose role will be to run the configuration management function. The Configuration Manager will play a leading role in the planning and implementation of configuration management and will probably be appointed as the manager of the planning and implementation project. Please see Annex C for a suggested job description and also section 3.3.2.

The IT Directorate staff described in sections 3.3.3 to 3.3.4 and senior user managers are candidates for inclusion in the project team(s).

3.1 Procedures

Once appointed, the Configuration Manager with the project team, must carry out the following activities.

3.1.1 Agree objectives

The scope and objectives of the configuration management function may well have been defined in the IS strategy. Agreement should be reached with senior IT management on whether the configuration management function is to be responsible for all phases of the application lifecycle (as recommended in this module) or whether there are to be separate configuration management functions for the IT infrastructure/operational service and the various system development projects. This module covers IT infrastructure configuration management only. A decision should be taken on the breadth and depth of the coverage of the IT infrastructure, but that can probably be deferred until planning gets under way (see 3.1.4 and 3.1.5).

There should be an agreement on whether configuration management is to include or is to work alongside change management, and on the extent to which SC&D, hardware installation and acceptance, management of local processors and terminals and other IT Infrastructure Library disciplines are to be included in the responsibilities of the configuration management team. For guidance on the planning of these functions, please see the appropriate modules of the IT Infrastructure Library.

The IT Services Manager, perhaps in collaboration with other IT managers including more senior ones, should draft an overall objective for the configuration management function, to be discussed and agreed by the Configuration Manager.

The objective might be:

> "to bring all IT infrastructure components and associated items of documentation under ongoing configuration management control and thereby to facilitate the management of change and the handling of incidents and problems and in general to contribute to the economic provision of quality IT services in the face of changing business and user requirements".

Detailed objectives include:

* recording the names and versions of the physical items that make up the IT infrastructure and the relationships between them (eg A is used by B; C is connected to D; E is a part of F; etc) and the required 'attributes' of the items

* making sure all changes to the IT infrastructure are properly authorized and, once implemented, are recorded immediately

* identifying the current status and the recent history of all items on the IT infrastructure

* identifying and storing definitive authorized and trusted copies of software

    - for distribution and use

    - as a basis for future development work

    - to be reverted to in an emergency

* identifying and storing definitive authorized specifications of items to be bought or developed

* checking the actual state of the IT infrastructure corresponds to the authorized state.

Certain of the objectives involve the procedures defined in the **Change Management** and **Software Control & Distribution** modules as well as this module.

3.1.2 Staff recruitment

The Configuration Manager must estimate the number of support staff required and instigate their recruitment or transfer. Guidance on the factors to be taken into account to decide staff numbers and some practical examples are described in section 3.3.3. Sections 3.3.5 and 3.3.6 give advice on recruitment and training respectively.

Staff numbers should be reviewed and, if necessary, amended as planning and implementation proceed; and subsequently in the light of experience with the ongoing running of configuration management.

3.1.3 Awareness campaign

The use of configuration management within IT is still relatively new. The Configuration Manager should plan and execute an awareness campaign aimed at everyone who will have dealings with the new configuration management function, to inform them of what is involved and how they will be affected (see section 3.3). This campaign may consist of visits or presentations to individual staff members, group seminars, leaflets or circulars. The function will have more chance of success if those using it have conviction that it will provide the organization with real benefits, rather than reluctance because it has been decreed, apparently arbitrarily, from above. Make it clear in the awareness campaign that there is senior management commitment to configuration management - invite senior management to give the opening address at seminars, to sign leaflets and in general 'to lead from the front'.

At an early stage in the planning of configuration management it will be possible to give information to affected people only in general terms. Subsequently, all concerned should be made clearly aware of their revised roles and responsibilities and detailed training should be given in the new procedures.

3.1.4 Plan scope of items to be controlled

The organization must decide what components of the IT infrastructure are to be controlled. Hardware, communications equipment, software and the documentation associated with these items should certainly be included. Accommodation and/or environmental components associated with the IT infrastructure should also be included. Computer centre facilities, telecommunications services and other items can be included.

Records of current and planned standards for hardware such as terminals and PCs should be stored as CIs. Individual items of such hardware are identified by having different serial numbers. Records of the definitive copy of each software item for distribution should be stored as CIs and the distributed copies identified as being related to the definitive copy.

A mechanism for associating Requests For Change (RFCs), Incident Records (IRs), Problem Records (PRs) and Known Error Records (KERs) with the IT infrastructure CIs to which they refer is required, and all these relationships should be included in and available from the CMDB. Records of requests for change and of changes authorized will be stored as CIs. A mechanism for storing records for package releases (implemented and authorized) as CIs is required. RFC, change and package release records must identify the IT infrastructure CIs affected. These records must also identify the make-up of the changes. See section 3.1.11 for further details.

The relationships between CIs must be stored; for example:

* a CI is a **part** of another CI (eg a software module is part of a program) - this as a parent/child relationship

* a CI is **connected** to another CI (eg a terminal is connected to a LAN)

* a CI **uses** another CI (eg a program uses a module from another program).

Some organizations may wish to use the CMDB to store and control details of the IT users and/or internal IT staff and perhaps also organizational structure. (Note that the Data Protection Act would apply in these cases). Such information would allow personnel changes to be related to changes in CI ownership.

Another use for the CMDB is to store inventory details of CIs such as supplier, cost, purchase date, renewal date for licence or maintenance contract, etc.

It is advisable to implement configuration management gradually - starting with those types of CI, or with those parts of the IT infrastructure, where control is perceived as most important or in the greatest need of improvement, and then expanding the system to encompass other areas.

Plans for implementing configuration management should include a schedule of 'take on' of IT infrastructure parts and of CI types.

3.1.5 Plan Configuration Item (CI) level

A decision must be made on the level to which CIs will be identified and hence controlled. Try to decide in advance the lowest CI level that will be required, even if you do not immediately populate the CMDB down to this level. It will be worthwhile spending time on this activity and being as forward looking as possible. This may save costly reorganizations of the CMDB in the future. However, deciding the right level of CIs in advance is not always easy; if possible, obtain a configuration management support tool that does not unduly constrain further breakdown of CIs to lower level ones.

Figure 2: Example CI breakdown

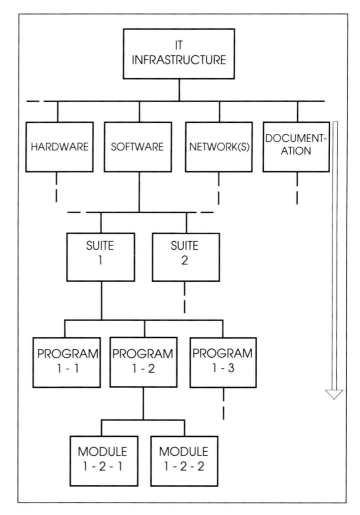

View the entire IT infrastructure as the highest level CI and then break it down into lower levels (see figure 2 for a simple example). Normally it is sufficient to go down only to the level of the smallest unit that is, in the normal course of events, independently installed, replaced or modified.

For further guidance and a more complex example please see section 3.1.7.

Choosing the right CI level is a matter of achieving a balance between information availability and the resources and effort needed to support it. For example if a change is to be made to module 1-2-2, it is better to record the change at module rather than program level - but it will be more costly to populate and maintain the CMDB down to module level.

On the other hand, actual changes must be made at the level recorded in the CMDB - so if it has been decided that the CMDB will record software at program level, changes must be made at this level (eg if a single module is to be changed it will be necessary to recompile the whole program to make the change at program level).

Many CIs (eg release packages, application software suites) are assemblies of lower level CIs (eg programs, modules).

Where the same lower level CI is a component of more that one higher level CI - for example, a software module that is used in different programs - it is highly advisable to populate the CMDB down to the level of the 'component' CI (the common module, in this example). Continuing this example, if a different physical copy of the module is used in different programs, the modules are replicated in the CMDB to reflect the copies, and each program is represented as a hierarchy of modules in parent/child relationships.

Although a child CI must be 'owned' by one parent CI, it can be 'used by' any number of other CIs.

If information at a low CI level would not be valuable - for example on PC keyboards if they are not usually exchanged independently - do not store it! CI information is valuable only if it facilitates the management of change, the control of incidents and problems, or the control of assets that can be independently moved, copied or changed.

The organization should plan to review the CI level on a regular basis - is information down to a low level still valuable and useful? Are the handling of changes and problems and the management of assets deficient because the CMDB does not go to a sufficiently low level? See also section 5.1.4.

3.1.6 Variants

Although the same CI can be used in more than one 'place' on an IT infrastructure, it is quite possible to use a slightly different version of what could otherwise be regarded as the same CI. This slightly different version would have a different version number (see section 3.1.11). Such CIs are called variants.

To appreciate how variants can be useful, consider a very simple example of an aeroplane with a type number of 555. A different type of engine is fitted to a number of 555 planes. If the planes with the new engine are regarded as different types of aeroplane and given a type number of 565 then the relationships between the other components which are common to all planes are not immediately identifiable. If at some future date a design fault is found in the wings of a 555 plane necessitating recall of all planes of this type, the fact that the same wings are also fitted to 565 planes will not be so obvious and may be overlooked. If instead the planes with the new engines had been regarded as variants of the 555 type and called, for example, 555As, this oversight would not have occurred.

Note, however, that if the wings themselves had been under configuration management control - ie configuration management control at a lower CI level - there would be no danger of failing to identify planes at risk, whatever their type number.

For a further example, this time more related to IT infrastructure management, consider a computer with two floppy disc drives A and B, both initially version 1.1. If B is modified to increase the capacity and data transfer rate, it becomes 1.1.1. Drive A could be left unmodified to retain backwards compatibility. If a design fault is subsequently found in A and is corrected (taking A to 1.2), this change must be propagated to B (taking it to 1.2.1). A and B **could** be regarded as different, unrelated CIs. However, it can be advantageous, because they share a large number of common components, to regard one as a variant of the other. Another and very common example of the use of variants is where a 'standard' system is 'customized' for particular applications.

The organization must decide whether it will allow the use of variants, or make it mandatory that all changes to a CI must result in the creation of a completely new CI.

There is normally a trade-off involved. The use of variants can result in fewer CIs to manage and may make it easier to identify items for commonality of treatment, be this in error-handling or for the implementation of changes. The use of variants will, however, introduce extra complexity to the configuration management system and/or any systems such as problem management that rely on it.

General guidance is: if a CI can be regarded as slightly different from another related CI, and problems affecting one are likely to affect the other, or changes made to the one will probably have to be made to the other, then use of a variant may be considered. Otherwise a different CI should be used.

3.1.7 Representation of hardware, software and networks

Distributed systems

A distributed IT system can be represented in the CMDB in a number of ways.

It would be ideal to have a configuration management tool that allows the configuration to be defined and presented graphically, but such tools are not yet generally available.

The following simple example is used to demonstrate possible ways in which hardware, software and network CIs can be represented in the CMDB.

**Figure 3:
Example
configuration**

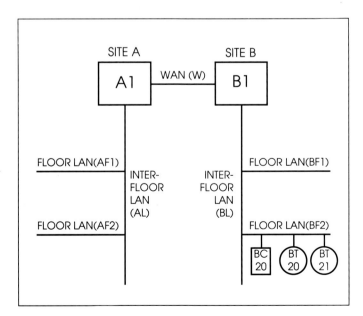

Figure 3 shows a simple configuration diagram which consists of two sites A and B which have mainframe computers A1 and B1 respectively. These are connected via a Wide Area Network (WAN) which is identified as W.

Each site has an inter-floor Local Area Network (LAN), identified as AL and BL respectively. To each of these are connected floor LANs - AF1 and AF2 are connected to AL, while BF1 and BF2 are connected to BL.

Connected to floor LAN BF2 are a minicomputer, BC20, and terminals BT20 and BT21 (in reality there would probably be many components connected to each floor LAN but these have been omitted for clarity).

To represent this configuration, start at the highest level with the whole IT infrastructure, referred to in this example as IX. Figure 4 shows that IX is represented as the parent of the WAN, the mainframes and the interfloor LANs.

**Figure 4:
High-level
breakdown**

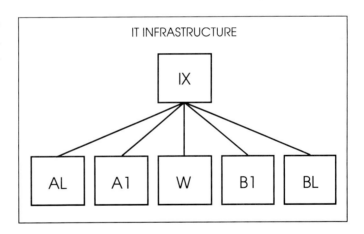

Figure 5 (overleaf) shows how the inter-floor LAN, BL, is represented as the parent of floor LANs BF1 and BF2 (AL would be the parent of AF1 and AF2). It also shows how BF2 is represented as the parent of the mini computer BC20 and the terminals BT20 and BT21.

As BC20 allows terminals BT20 and BT21 to access other computers via the LANs and the WAN, 'access' relationships would also have to be shown.

The software resident on this configuration would be shown as a separate hierarchy but relationships between the software and the hardware have to be made. A 'resident on'

Figure 5:
Parent-child
relationships

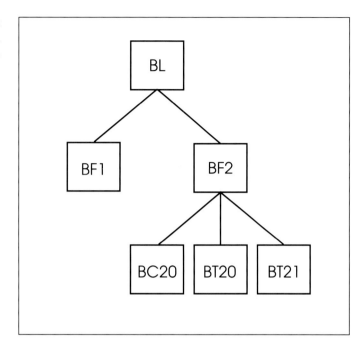

relationship would be established for the software that resides on the mainframes, the mini and the local terminals (if any).

Where it would be useful, 'access' relationships can be established between the terminals or terminal users and the software they are able to access (eg on computers to which they are not directly connected).

If standard software configurations ('sets') are used (eg all the terminals on a nationwide network have access to identical software sets), then these sets can be defined and 'access' relationships established to the sets. This can considerably reduce the number of relationships that are needed compared with when individual software CIs relationships are used.

External networks

In cases where a network is regarded as part of, or is used by, the IT infrastructure, but cannot be brought under configuration management control, for example an external Wide Area Network (WAN) owned by another organization, the network can be represented as a single high-level CI with all connections to the network represented as 'used by' or 'connected to' relationships.

Figure 6 shows how these relationships might be defined.

Figure 6:
External network
connections

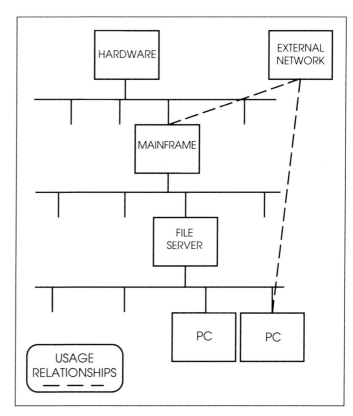

3.1.8 Model, version and copy numbers

When a CI is amended or altered in some way, it is usual for it to retain the same CI name, but its version number must be changed. A decision must be made on the numbering convention to be used for versions - a 2 or 3 level number is recommended with the top level reserved for major changes and the bottom level for small changes.

For hardware changes, it is usual to increment the minor version number for changes that either do not affect functionality, or affect it only in a small way. If variants are allowed, the minor version number can be used for them.

Major changes in hardware functionality can be represented by a new 'model' number - for example, a PC with a new, faster processor could retain the same CI name but receive a different model number. A change of model number in this context corresponds to a 'very major' version change. Model numbers can be aligned to suppliers' model numbers.

Different instances of the same CI whether copies of
software or separate items of hardware all to the same
specification should be distinguished by means of 'copy
numbers' or 'serial numbers'. These numbers need to be
distinguished from the version number which indicates a
change from a previous version.

3.1.9 Plan naming conventions

The Configuration Manager must arrange for a naming
convention to be established for all CIs. Individual instances
of CIs must be uniquely identifiable by means of the CIs
name and copy/serial number.

Note that the version number identifies a changed version
of what can be regarded as the same CI. More than one
version of the same CI can coexist at the same time.

A variant can have the same name as its 'near relative', but
should have a different version number. To distinguish
different copies of the same variant a different copy number
must be used.

Figure 7: Terminal breakdown

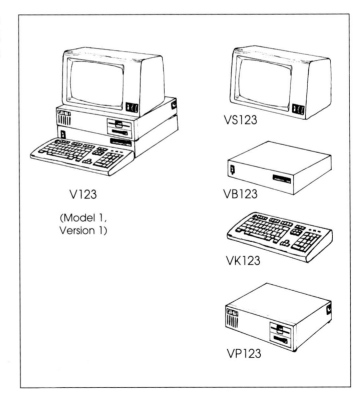

V123

(Model 1, Version 1)

VS123

VB123

VK123

VP123

When the naming convention is being planned it is very important that sufficient account is taken of possible future growth. It is not appropriate to lay down specific conventions in this module, but the following points are worth considering:

* keep names relatively short

* make them as meaningful as possible

* utilize any suitable existing conventions with which staff are already familiar.

Figure 7 gives a very simple example. If hardware terminals are already given identifiers from an allocated range of numbers V001 to V999 (which in this case already has sufficient spare numbers to accommodate future growth), use this as a basis for the CI identifiers (ie CI name, serial number). Terminal V123 might consist of a VDU screen, badge reader, processor and keyboard and these could be identified as VS123, VB123, VP123 and VK123 respectively. V, VS, VB, VP and VK are the CI names and 123 is the serial number of each CI.

Figure 8:
Version change

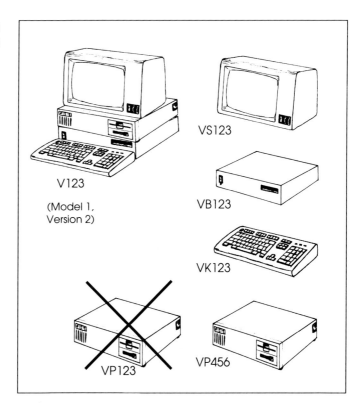

VS123

V123

(Model 1,
Version 2)

VB123

VK123

VP123

VP456

Figure 8 (page 23) uses the same example to show how version and model numbers can be used. Terminal V123 is a model 1 terminal, which can be regarded as an assembly, consisting of VS123, VB123, VP123 and VK123. No previous changes have been made to this terminal, so it can be regarded as version 1.0. The processor fails and is replaced by, say, VP456 (an identical processor with a different serial number). Although the functionality is unchanged, it is still desirable to record the processor change (eg for contractual or problem trending purposes). This can be achieved by incrementing the version number of terminal V123 to version 2. The terminal remains a model 1, because there has been no change at all in functionality.

Figure 9 shows a different type of change. A model 1 terminal, V123, version 1.0 is an assembly which consists of VS123, VB123, VP123 and VK123. The processor VP123 is replaced by a more powerful version XP123. Because this replacement results in a major change in functionality the change must be reflected in another manner and so V123 becomes a model 2 terminal. The CI identifier (name and serial number) remains as V123, as the name must be constant to allow a complete CI history. Over a period of time all the components in the assembly may eventually be replaced and the model number and/or version number will be changed to reflect this, but the CI name and serial number will always remain the same while the CI is to be regarded as 'the same terminal'.

For hardware, if the CI naming and numbering conventions are not based on suppliers' device names and serial numbers, a mechanism must be set up to relate configuration management and suppliers' identifiers to each other - for example, for the convenience of hardware engineers.

Although each CI must be uniquely identified by its name and serial/copy number, a CI can exist as part of any number of different CIs or CI sets at the same time. For instance, VK123 in the example above is a part of V123, but it can also be regarded as one of many keyboards of a particular model and one of many hardware items purchased from a particular supplier or on a particular date (provided such attributes of the CI have been recorded in the CMDB - see 3.1.10).

Release records, change records and other CIs that are 'associated with' the IT infrastructure, all need CI identifiers.

Figure 9:
Model change

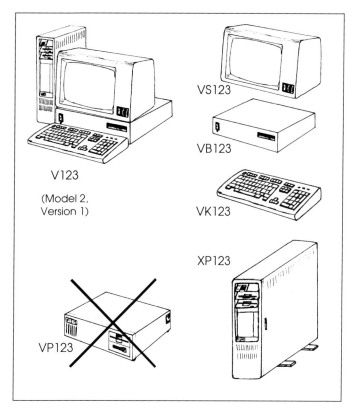

A simple numbering scheme, such as R1, R2, R3, R4, ... is recommended, with version numbers used to indicate changes, for example to release plans.

3.1.10 Plan attributes to be recorded for CIs

The Configuration Manager must plan which attributes are to be recorded. As the required attributes may vary for different categories or types of CI, consideration should be given to only current and forecast CI types. To some extent; the decision may be influenced by the support tool(s) used. Annex B gives a suggested list of attributes which should be recorded if possible, but this may need modification to meet local requirements, or to comply with support tool facilities.

When the attributes to be recorded have been decided, plan how to obtain the necessary data. Except for greenfield systems, most of this data will already exist within the organization. It will however need to be extracted. This may be a large, difficult and time-consuming task.

3.1.11 Relationship with change and problem management

Configuration management facilitates the control of changes to the IT infrastructure. Whenever a change is requested, an RFC record is raised, which documents which IT infrastructure CIs are to be affected and how. Once the change has been authorized, the RFC becomes a change record or release record, which documents the effect of the change on IT infrastructure CIs, and indicates a reversion path and the consequences of revision. At each stage the configuration management records for affected CIs should be updated with the number of the RFC or change record cancelled.

The CMDB must hold information on current and previous versions of CIs, and on their current status. Planned future CIs and CI versions, including software-package releases, as scheduled by change management should also be recorded.

The status of CIs in the CMDB should be changed as these items progress from 'ordered' or development to test, to live, and to archive. A 'scheduled status' indicator, to show a planned future status-change is useful. Such an indicator should be accompanied by a date or other indication of when the change is scheduled to take place.

It is quite possible for a child CI to have a different status from one or more of its parents. For example, a module of software could be current even though it was designed as part of a version of a program that is now superseded.

Plans should be made to log the status of IT infrastructure CIs as follows:

new CIs

* CI under development or being procured

existing CIs

* RFC raised on this CI: a new version of the CI (possibly with some new children or different child versions) is being requested

* RFC authorized and change scheduled: a new version of the CI is to be created and will be implemented as part of a scheduled change or release; a change or release record - itself a CI - documents all CIs/CI versions to be included in the change or release and the CIs that will be superseded

(normally all the CIs belonging to the previous release will be superseded, although component CIs may be retained in the new release); the change or release record also documents the make up and effect of the planned change and indicates a reversion path and the consequences of reversion

all CIs

* item is procured or change release is built: status of change or release record and of records for affected IT infrastructure CIs changes to reflect progress during the build or procurement

* item or release is tested: change or release record indicates items for test; during testing the change or release record, and component records for affecting IT infrastructure CIs are changed to show how testing is progressing

* item or release goes live: change or release record indicates items for live use; once item or release goes live, status of release record and records for affected IT infrastructure CIs is changed to 'live'. Records for superseded CIs are changed to show that they have been archived.

Note that RFC and change records are themselves subject to change/configuration management control and therefore may not be changed without authorization.

Figure 10 (overleaf) shows, in simplified form, the relationship between the various stages in problem and change management.

In this example an incident occurs which shows that there is a problem; the cause of the problem is then diagnosed and the problem becomes a known error. This error is corrected by implementing a change, probably via a package release.

To facilitate the problem and change management processes and to build up a valuable source of management information, the cross-relationships between incidents, problems, known errors, changes, and the IT infrastructure CIs to which they refer should be available in the CMDB.

Problem management procedures must therefore ensure that each time an incident, problem or known error arises the identification number of the incident, problem or known error is recorded against affected CIs in the CMDB,

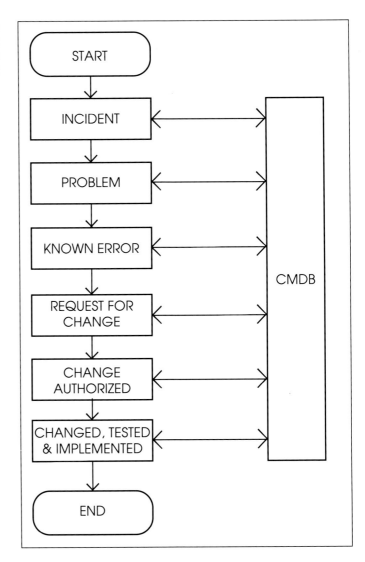

**Figure 10:
Interfaces to
problem and change
management**

provided that a configuration management tool is chosen which allows this. The incident, problem and known error records should list the IT infrastructure CIs affected and state how they are affected.

Where existing problem and change management systems have been implemented without configuration management, those systems should be integrated into the new configuration management system. It is recommended that change management is made part of configuration management.

For further information please see the **Change Management** and **Problem Management** modules.

3.1.12 Planning of baselines

It is useful to treat certain CIs as baselines. A baseline is a snapshot of the state of a CI and its component CIs, at a point in time. A baseline is normally created for one of two reasons:

*   as a sound basis for future work (establishing a point in the life of a CI from which you can progress)

*   as a point you can retreat to if things go wrong.

Baselines are subject to configuration management actions such as:

*   revert system to previous baseline (the effect that reversion will have should be clearly recorded in the CMDB)

*   update system from current baseline

*   buy hardware according to current baseline

*   copy software and documentation at current baseline, to all remote sites.

In general baselines correspond or are related to CI types previously described in this module, and include:

*   package release records (current, past and planned)

*   other change records (current, past and planned)

*   the state of a system and its documentation when a change or package release is (or will be) applied

*   hardware - standard specifications.

Current baselines should either physically exist in a form that can be easily worked on or reverted to, or should be capable of being easily built using procedures and components that are under configuration management control. Specific examples of the use of baselines include:

*   as a particular 'standard' configuration item, needed when buying many items of the same type (eg PCs) over a protracted period. If some PCs are to include additional printed circuit boards this could correspond to 'baseline plus'. If all future PCs are to have these boards, a new baseline is created

*   as a trusted state of, for example a software release to be reverted to (must exist physically and be capable of easy reversion)

* as the state of software for distribution to remote sites

* as the state of software to be worked on in the future

* as the state a system **must** be in before it can be upgraded to accept specified new hardware or software.

The planning activities required for baselines include identifying what baselines are going to be required and for what purposes, deciding the configuration management actions allowed on them, estimating how many versions of baselines will exist concurrently and the frequency of baseline changes, and deciding the naming conventions.

As baselines are themselves CIs, their names should follow the agreed CI naming conventions.

Several baselines corresponding to different stages in the life of the 'baselined item' concerned exist at any given time. For example, the baseline for the software release that is currently live, the one that was last live and has now been archived, the one that will next be installed (subject to change under configuration management control), and one or more under test.

If, for instance, new software is being introduced gradually on a regional basis, more than one version of a baseline could be 'live' at the same time. It is therefore best to refer to each by a unique version number, rather than 'live', 'next' etc.

3.1.13 Plan support tools

The Configuration Manager must evaluate available support tools and instigate procurement of the selected tool and any necessary hardware on which to run the tool. This is a very important activity because the nature of the support tool(s) could heavily influence the operation of the configuration management function. Provision must be made in financial estimates for the costs of tools and hardware (Government Departments should include these as early as possible in supply estimates). Account should be taken of delivery lead times.

Section 7 describes configuration management tool requirements and gives examples of tools currently available.

3.1.14 Plan registration of Configuration Items

Procedures must be established for 'registering' existing and new CIs (entering them and their attributes in the CMDB and bringing them under configuration management control). The registration of existing CIs is covered in section 3.1.15. This section deals with the registration of new CIs.

Control must be established for new CIs no later than the point when they are 'delivered' into the operational environment.

The way in which the status of CIs changes as they progress from delivery to live use, and the handling of CI changes and releases, are discussed in section 3.1.11. Ideally the CMDB should be updated automatically as the status of CIs and releases changes.

Software developed in-house

For software developed in-house the point of 'delivery' is normally the point at which software is ready for operational acceptance. The **Software Control & Distribution** module recommends the use of a Definitive Software Library (DSL), where all software CIs (including documentation in electronic form) are held in their definitive, quality-controlled state. Registration procedures must ensure that details of all authorized software and supporting documentation CIs are entered in the CMDB before the CIs are transferred from the development library into the DSL. The status of the CIs should be altered when they enter the DSL (eg from 'planned' to 'present'). Ideally the CMDB update should be carried out automatically by the utility program or support tool that does the physical library transfer. Unauthorized items must not be allowed in the DSL.

For software CIs that have been configuration-managed during their development stages using the same CMDB, only a status change, rather than a new entry, may need to be made initially. If a shared database is used for development and live CIs, access controls should be applied to limit access to only the appropriate staff - eg development staff have access only to development CIs. If a different tool or database has been used the CI data must be transferred into the new CMDB. Ideally the CI data should not need re-keying.

Bought-in
Configuration Items

Procedures must be planned for bought-in CIs, including hardware, communications equipment, documentation, software packages, operating systems software and utilities. Goods-inward procedures covering computer operations, network management, computer installation/acceptance, procurement and administrative staff must ensure that all authorized new CIs are correctly registered in the CMDB before they are delivered and that the status of theses CIs is changed as they are delivered, installed, tested, accepted, etc. A check must be made that delivered CIs are authorized. Installation procedures must not commence until this check has been satisfactorily carried out. Further details are available in the **Software Control & Distribution**, **Computer Installation & Acceptance**, **Network Management** and **Management of Local Processors & Terminals** modules.

3.1.15 Plan population of CMDB

Plans must be made for the initial population of the CMDB, to reflect the current state of the IT infrastructure. To establish an accurate picture of the state of CIs, a complete inventory of all CIs must be planned. The CMDB should be populated as the inventory is carried out. Ideally the state of CIs should be 'frozen' during CMDB population, but this may not be practical. However, once configuration management data is captured for particular CIs, these CIs should be bought immediately under configuration management control. In that case, it may be possible to popuiate the CMDB in a phased way (eg start with the hardware and then gradually progress to software, networks etc).

If it is not possible to bring items under configuration management control as the inventory is taken, plans must be made for procedures to track and record any changes that occur between the time the inventory is taken and the start of configuration management control (eg when CMDB population is complete).

The registration procedures for new CIs, mentioned in section 3.1.14, should be brought into effect as soon as possible, preferably before the data on existing CIs is collected.

For large IT systems already in existence, a significant amount of data entry may be required to populate the CMDB. Although this work can be a chore, the benefits of having CI data under management control are such that the investment quickly pays for itself. Consideration should be given to the temporary use of skilled data entry staff for this task, though if time allows it may be an opportunity for configuration management staff to become familiar with the support tool. If any of the data is already electronically stored for other purposes, consideration should be given to reformatting and transferring the data.

3.1.16 Plan the labelling of CIs

All CIs must be labelled with the CI name, a model number and version number, copy/serial number as appropriate, so that they can be easily identified. Plans must be made to label CIs and to maintain the accuracy of their labels.

Hardware

Physical labels must be attached to all hardware CIs. All cables/lines should be clearly labelled at each end and at any inspection points.

It is advisable to use a standard format and colour for all such labels, as this makes it easier for users to identify and quote from them, eg when ringing the Help Desk to report a fault.

Software

Definitive copies of software must be held in the DSL and must not be issued to anyone. Where possible, all copies of software should have a software label containing the CI name copy number and version number at the head/start of the file. All media containing software should be clearly labelled with the CI name, copy number and version number of each of the software items contained on the media (as well as the CI name and serial number of the media itself).

Documentation

Definitive copies of documentation should **never** be issued, but should be retained in a documentation library. Unregistered copies of documents should not be allowed. To avoid the inadvertent use of obsolete documents, steps should be taken to detect or eliminate any unregistered copies. Thus all copies of documents should be marked with a coloured label (coloured as the colour is difficult to photocopy) containing the CI name copy and version numbers. Numbered copies can then be issued to registered users, who have to confirm they have received their copy and destroyed any superseded documents - so you know who has got each copy. If a document will change at some known future date, then a shelf-life date could also be included (eg "the contents of this document are not valid after 1 September 1992").

Documentation held in electronic form should have a software label as described in 'software', above.

Other CIs

CIs that exist in any other form should, so far as possible, be labelled. For example an RFC screen can be labelled if a computer-based system is used.

3.1.17 Consider distribution of control

If the configuration management system is to control a distributed IT infrastructure with many locations, consideration should be given to distributing configuration management control. Although a single centralized CMDB is essential, in certain circumstances better physical control of CIs may be possible by having configuration management staff on-site at remote locations. In such cases remote access, via an integrated configuration management tool, to a centralized CMDB is essential.

3.1.18 Devise implementation plan

Once the fundamental decisions on the scope of configuration management have been taken and the planning activities described in previous subsections have been carried out, a plan for implementing configuration management must be devised. For guidance on what this plan should include, please refer to section 4.1.

3.1.19 Plan the ongoing management and operation

Plans must be made for the ongoing operation and management of configuration management. Much of the planning has already been covered in previous sub-sections.

Ongoing procedures include:

* managing change, including

    - registration of all new CIs

    - deletion of withdrawn/terminated CIs (it may be decided, however, that the CMDB should contain historic records of CIs that no longer actually exist that, depending on the CI type, go back a predefined number of versions, or for a predetermined period of time)

    - updating of the CMDB to reflect all status changes that occur to CIs (eg development to test, test to live, live to archive)

    - use of the CMDB to facilitate impact assessment of RFCs, to define changes to be implemented, to record the effect of expected changes, to document backout actions and forecast effects, and to maintain an accurate record of the system when changes are implemented

- in general, controlling IT assets - see also 3.1.11

* maintenance of hardware standards, master copies of documents etc. under configuration management control (see 3.1.12)

* provision of CMDB to assist with incident and problem handling (see 3.1.11)

* regular checking of the status of the CMDB against the installed system and implementing any corrective action (see 3.1.20)

* providing and supporting the provision of management information on CIs (eg on the extent to which problems and errors are affecting which CIs; on life-expiry dates, licence fee renewal dates and costs, etc)

* reviewing configuration management for efficiency and effectiveness, reporting to management and taking any necessary corrective action (see 3.1.21)

* ensuring the configuration management system is aware and capable of coping with future workloads and growth (eg that adequate staff and IT resources are provided for configuration management).

For further information, please see also section 5.1.

3.1.20 Configuration auditing

Plans must be made for regular configuration audits to check that the CMDB is consistent with the physical state of all CIs and vice-versa.

These audits should verify that correct and authorized versions of CIs exist, and that **only** such CIs exist, and are in use in the operational environment. From the outset, any ad-hoc tools, test equipment, personal computers and other 'non-registered' items must either be removed or registered through formal configuration management. Non-registered and unauthorized items that 'turn up' during configuration audits must be investigated, and corrective action instigated to procedures, and if appropriate to the behaviour of personnel.

Plans should be laid down to carry out configuration audits:

* shortly after implementation of the new configuration management system (population of the CMDB gives a good opportunity to determine the physical inventory)

* before and after major changes to the IT infrastructure

* should a disaster occur - upon detection of the disaster to establish which CIs have been lost or damaged, and following 'return to normal' to ensure the integrity of the CMDB (this should be included in contingency plans)

* at random intervals.

Note that the insertion of 'Trojan Horses', 'trap doors' and 'viruses' through collusion, is discouraged when the configuration management team is seen to be in control and to carry out regular and frequent audits.

In addition, the Help Desk must be instructed to check that CIs brought to its attention (eg the terminal and software that a caller is using when they telephone to report an incident) are as recorded in the CMDB and to report any deviations to configuration management for investigation.

If an epidemic of unauthorized CIs is detected, selective or general configuration audits should be instigated to determine the scale of the problem, to put matters right, and to discourage a proliferation of unauthorized CIs.

3.1.21 Reviewing and auditing the configuration management function

Plan to review the configuration management function regularly for efficiency and effectiveness. Regular audits of the configuration management function, to check for compliance with the procedures described in this module, should also be planned.

Configuration management underpins a number of other IT infrastructure management functions such as change management, problem management, and the Help Desk. In some instances these functions may have been implemented before configuration management. Whether or not this is so, it will be necessary to carry out a wide-ranging assessment of the state of IT infrastructure management before and after configuration management is introduced, in order to gauge the impact of configuration management.

To show the way in which configuration management facilitates the management of change, the handling of problems, the control of IT assets - and to demonstrate its effectiveness in improving the quality of IT services - the following information should be determined and recorded:

* the number of changes per month that are implemented without the required authorization

* the number of changes per month that have to be withdrawn because they contain errors

* the impact on the IT services of changes implemented without the required authorization

* the impact on the IT services of changes that have to be withdrawn because they contain errors

* the number of occasions when the 'configuration' is not as authorized and the impact on the IT services, the IT budget, and the legality of the organization of such deviations

* the average amount of time it takes to perform an impact assessment following a Request For Change (RFC)

* the average cost of performing such an assessment

* the number and seriousness of incidents and problems per month

* the number and seriousness of incidents and problems that can be traced back to wrongly made changes

* the proportion of Help Desk calls that are received per month that are resolved whilst the user is on the telephone, without the need for further escalation

* the average time and cost of diagnosing and resolving Help Desk calls that cannot be resolved immediately

* the number and seriousness of occasions when service level agreements have been breached, when the problem can be traced back to errors made in the change management, problem management or Help Desk functions

* the number and value of unauthorized IT assets detected in use.

A before-and-after assessment should show an improvement in these measures, and there should be a gradual and continuous improvement once configuration management is in operation.

IT Services Management is responsible for reviewing trends and instigating any necessary corrective action.

Please see sections 5.1.5 and 5.1.6 for further details of these reviews and audits.

3.2 Dependencies

3.2.1 Supporting disciplines

Configuration management is heavily dependent upon a number of other disciplines. In particular, effective change management and software control & distribution (SC&D) functions (both often regarded as part of configuration management), operational acceptance testing, and procedures for the installation and acceptance of new/ different hardware and network components, are essential. If these are not already in existence, they must be planned alongside configuration management. Effective problem management procedures are also highly desirable to reap most benefit from configuration management. If no problem management procedures exist, consideration should be given to planning such procedures as soon as possible.

3.2.2 Support tools

For all but the smallest systems, configuration management support tools are essential, as paper based systems are impractical. Computer hardware and storage resources are required to accommodate such tools and, in particular, the CMDB.

If support tools are purchased or developed for the configuration management group, those tools should also be brought under configuration management control procedures. Section 7 describes tool requirements.

Support tools should, as a minimum, allow data to be transferred from separate 'project configuration management' systems without the need for re-keying. Ideally the configuration management tools for the 'live system' and for 'projects' should work together in an integrated way.

3.2.3 Finance and administration

There should be strong ties with the Finance and Administration Section (FAS).

CIs are the organization's property, whether they are hardware, software, documents, or anything else. The Configuration Management Group is responsible for making FAS aware of any changes in the location and condition of this property.

Approval to pay for IT infrastructure components should involve verification by the Configuration Management Group that those CIs have actually been received, have been installed, and are working correctly.

3.2.4 Management and staff commitment

The long term commitment of management and staff is required for configuration management to work effectively.

3.3 People

The key people involved during the planning stages are described in sections 3.3.1 to 3.3.4.

3.3.1 The IT Services Manager

The IT Services Manager is the head of the IT Services Section and has overall responsibility for service quality. Typically his/her peer managers are the Applications Development Manager(s) and the Finance & Administration Manager (see figure 11).

The IT Services Manager must initiate the whole process of installing a configuration management function and take overall responsibility for winning the hearts and minds of personnel who will be affected by configuration management.

Figure 11: Management structure

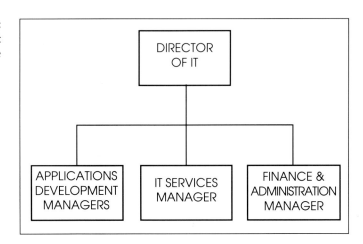

3.3.2 The Configuration Manager

The Configuration Manager is appointed by and reports to, the IT Services Manager. The Configuration Manager is responsible for configuration management when it is implemented and will play a leading role - probably as project manager - on the configuration management development and implementation project. A suggested job description for the Configuration Manager is given at Annex C.

Change management and software control & distribution are covered in separate IT Infrastructure Library modules. However, it is recommended that where possible these activities are combined with that of configuration management and carried out by a Configuration Management Group, headed by the Configuration Manager. Optionally, this group may also be given responsibility for installation and acceptance of computer hardware and telecommunications network components.

3.3.3 Support staff

Configuration management support staff are required, other than in very small installations. It is not possible to give prescriptive guidance on staff numbers, but the following factors should be taken into account:

* whether the configuration group is to be responsible for development projects as well as the IT infrastructure

* whether the group is also to be responsible for change management and/or software control & distribution

* whether hardware/network installation and acceptance responsibilities are allocated to the group

* the size of the IT infrastructure, the level at which control is to be maintained, and hence the number of CIs to be controlled

* the extent to which support tools are available

* the size, frequency and complexity of software changes and releases and of changes to the hardware/communications equipment.

Configuration management is usually on the critical path between applications development and live operations. It is also involved in all changes to live hardware, software and networks; and provides information that is needed for the effective handling of problems.

There should therefore be enough trained staff to cover for annual leave and other absences. The minimum practical staffing level is at least two people - including the Configuration Manager - though where appropriate, such as in very small installations, one of these two could be a 'reserve'.

At the opposite end of the scale, the Inland Revenue, Telford has a team of 4-5 people carrying out their IT infrastructure configuration management and SC&D activities using a dedicated dual node ICL 3980 computer. Inland Revenue Telford also has a 4-5 person configuration management team in each of its applications development project groups. This gives a total of 20-25 staff employed on configuration management and SC&D duties but with a total IT workforce of approximately 1200 this represents only approximately 2% of staff.

Another example is the DSS/DE NUBS system which has 6 staff, out of a total of approximately 300, employed on configuration management and SC&D activities (covering both IT infrastructure management and application development projects).

3.3.4 Others involved

All staff who handover (to IT Services), accept, install or change any configuration items - including problem management, computer operations, network management, applications development, engineers, vendor and user staff and staff with responsibility for PCs, terminals and small computers - must do so only if change/configuration management authorization has been given and the CMDB has been updated with details of the new CI(s) or changes.

Procedural controls should be introduced to ensure that unauthorized change is virtually impossible.

3.3.5 Recruitment and retention of configuration management staff

If configuration management is being implemented into an existing system and some configuration management activities are already being carried out within other groups, try to recruit staff from these groups into the Configuration Management Group, even if only on a temporary basis until new staff are trained.

It is sometimes difficult to recruit and retain staff with the requisite skills because the work can be perceived as less interesting or creative than, for example, applications development. Potential recruits should be advised that the

Configuration Management Group occupies a pivotal role within IT services and offers exposure to, and opportunities to learn from, staff in many other IT groups.

3.3.6 Training

Staff should be given a programme consisting of on-the-job training and formal training courses. There should be formal training in the configuration management discipline and training should be given in the use of all support tools to be used. If suppliers of configuration management support tools or mainframe equipment suppliers offer configuration management training courses these should be considered for inclusion in the programme.

If the configuration management role is to be combined with that of change management and SC&D, training should be given in these disciplines, and in the use of support tools pertaining to them.

Configuration management staff should be given a general understanding of the hardware, software and telecommunications configuration over which they are to have configuration management control.

Training should be given in other responsibilities as appropriate.

It is useful to give configuration management staff an appreciation of the workings of the problem management and Help Desk systems, and of the way in which configuration management facilitates their operation.

3.3.7 Overtime and extended hours

In planning for the introduction of configuration management, IT Services management should consider the need for overtime or shift working.

When urgent releases or emergency fixes are required, the changes must always be subject to configuration management or change management control and must always be recorded in the CMDB. Whether or not change management is part of configuration management, the Configuration Management Group needs to arrange for its interests to be covered.

There are three options:

* provide staff at all hours

* make staff available on-call

* delegate authority to someone who is available (eg problem management or computer operations staff) - adequate procedures and training will be required.

This delegation must not under any circumstances be given to vendor or user staff.

3.3.8 Consultants

Where staff are not readily available, consider the use of consultants to perform configuration management activities until staff can be recruited and trained.

3.4 Timing

Organizations should begin planning for configuration management as soon as possible. It is estimated that the planning process could take anything from 4 to 12 months from inception to the point of implementation. This period could be considerably longer if finance is not readily available or there are long lead times for tools or equipment.

3.4.1 Finances

The staff, staff training, computer equipment and software support tools needed for configuration management should be included in future expenditure estimates (in the case of Government Departments, supply estimates) as soon as possible.

3.4.2 Lead time for training

Experience has shown that it takes at least one to two months for staff to complete training to the point where they can be effective.

Configuration management should not be implemented until the staff are adequately trained. If they try to take on control activities too soon, they may lose the co-operation of the other parts of the organization, by being perceived as a 'bottleneck'.

4. Implementation

This section deals with the implementation of the configuration management system.

4.1 Procedures

4.1.1 Installation and testing of support tool(s)

Configuration management support tool(s) must be installed and tested. Any problems identified must be rectified. Problems that are minor and would not affect the successful operation of the system need not be fixed before configuration management is implemented.

4.1.2 Completion of training

As soon as the support tools have been installed and are available for use, staff training in their use should be carried out. It may be possible to combine this training with the testing of the tools. Staff training in new procedures should be completed.

4.1.3 Publicize implementation

The Configuration Manager should publicize the implementation date and time for the new configuration management procedures. All people who are affected, in particular all IT Services staff and external suppliers and service providers, must be notified and must be reminded of their responsibility to adhere to the new procedures from the outset. See 3.3.4 for guidance on the parties affected most.

4.1.4 Populate the CMDB

The CMDB must be populated with details of the CIs to be included initially. For IT infrastructure CIs, the plans described in section 3.1.15 should therefore be implemented. If possible, CIs should be brought under configuration management control as soon as the CI data has been collected and no new items should be added to the IT infrastructure without coming under the control of configuration management (See 4.1.5). To reduce the need for manual work even if this is not possible, it is desirable to record changes that occur between collecting CI data, putting the data in the CMDB, and bringing the CIs under configuration management control. To do this, the time interval between these phases should be kept to a minimum for each CI.

Items such as RFCs, change records and release records corresponding to changes that are not yet implemented should be captured first. All RFCs from then on should be included on the CMDB. With this approach, the CMDB can be used to record all subsequent change activity, including authorization and implementation. The capture of any required historic records can be deferred until it is convenient.

4.1.5 Switch-over to new system

Provided all planning has been completed and the steps described in 4.1.1 to 4.1.3 have been carried out, the actual switch-over to the new configuration management system only requires people to start using the new procedures at the decided date and time.

This switch-over can take place in parallel with CMDB population, with CIs being gradually brought under configuration management control as the CI data is gathered and the information is recorded on the CMDB. Any changes to CIs that are not yet under configuration management control should be notified to the Configuration Management Group: if possible CIs affected by change should immediately be brought under configuration management control. All CIs that are new after the configuration management system has been switched on should be immediately brought under configuration management control.

In many cases procedural measures and the use of tools to automate some configuration management and software control & distribution processes can prevent, or at least detect, reversion to any previous procedures or practices.

Once the new configuration management system is in operation, it is vital that no new items are added to the IT infrastructure without configuration management authority. Existing items to which configuration management control applies (ie all CIs other than those temporarily excluded to accommodate a phased implementation) must not be changed without configuration management authorization. All unauthorized CIs/CI versions when detected must be either expunged or brought under configuration management control.

4.2 Dependencies

Ensure that planning described in 3.1 has been done and that the dependencies described in section 3.2 are in place prior to implementing configuration management.

4.3 People

The success of implementation depends on having enough trained staff. If the Configuration Management Group is understaffed or staffed by people who have not been adequately trained, it could become a bottleneck. Understaffing can also lead to critical errors which could cost more to put right than the cost of adequate staffing in the first place. Additional staff may be required for a short period at implementation time (eg to assist with the CI inventory and/or populating the CMDB).

Configuration management is important work which requires staff who will adopt a painstaking approach and pay due attention to detail.

Follow the recruitment and retention advice already provided in Section 3.3.

4.4 Timing

The most time-consuming part of the implementation is conducting the CI inventory and populating the CMDB. The amount of time this takes obviously depends on the size of the IT infrastructure and the number of CIs.

That apart, provided all planning tasks have been satisfactorily completed, this phase can be carried out relatively quickly.

Overall it is estimated that implementation of the configuration management system will take 1 to 3 months on average.

5. Post-implementation and audit

This section deals with the ongoing management and running of configuration management post-implementation.

5.1 Procedures

The primary responsibilities of the configuration management function are:

*   to provide a mechanism to ensure that all items on an IT infrastructure and all changes made to it are properly authorized

*   to ensure the CMDB, which reflects the authorized state of the IT infrastructure, is kept up to date in order to facilitate the management of change and the handling of problems and incidents.

The configuration management function is often combined with those of change management and SC&D. The Configuration Management Group may also be made responsible for installation and acceptance of new hardware and communications equipment. The day-to-day duties of the group therefore often incorporate these activities (see the separate **Change Management**, **Software Control & Distribution** and **Computer Installation & Acceptance** modules for details of these activities).

To ensure all items on an IT infrastructure are as authorized by change management, a record of all authorized changes and enhancements is made on the CMDB. The implementation of changes is done under configuration management control with actual changes carried out in accordance with the authorization record in the CMDB. Once a change is implemented the CMDB is amended to show the change in status of configuration items affected by the change.

Specific configuration management activity to ensure the CMDB is updated to reflect the actual state of the IT infrastructure may be triggered in the following ways:

*   when new CI(s) and new CI versions are added to the IT infrastructure

*   when the status of CI(s) changes (eg from 'live' to 'archive')

*   when the owner of CI(s) changes

* when the location of CI(s) changes

* when the relationships affecting CIs change

* when old CIs are removed from the IT infrastructure

* when an unregistered CI is detected, or when inaccurate CMDB information is found (eg when the Help Desk receives a call relating to an unregistered or inaccurately recorded CI; eg as a result of a configuration audit).

All IT Services staff should be alerted to report to configuration management any instances they detect of unauthorized CIs, or of CIs that do not match the information on the CMDB. Configuration management should trace the origin of each unregistered item, propose or initiate actions to register, correct, or expunge the CIs and to correct the deficiencies that allowed unregistered items to slip through, and report to management.

Sensitive handling may be required to avoid creating a 'black market' in unregistered CIs (eg unauthorized floppy discs).

5.1.1 Management reporting

Regular reports should be produced for management to show progress on the before-and-after configuration management metrics described in section 3.1.21. In addition, management reports should cover the following:

* results of configuration audits (see section 5.1.3)

* information on any non-registered or inaccurately-registered CIs that have been detected, and on corrective action

* information on the number of registered CIs/CI versions, broken down by CI category, type and status (possibly also location and other CI attributes)

* growth information (see also section 5.1.5)

* rate of change of CIs/CMDB

* details of any backlogs of configuration management work or any delays caused by configuration management activities, and proposed remedies

* configuration management staffing position

* amount of authorized work done out of hours by other IT services staff

* results of efficiency/effectiveness reviews, growth reviews and audits of the configuration management function (see sections 5.1.4 to 5.1.6), and proposals for tackling actual or potential problems.

As management information builds up on the CMDB, it will be available for interrogation and trend analysis by IT services management and other groups within IT Services such as problem management, change management, Help Desk and service level management staff.

For example, service level management staff may find that Service Level Agreements are not being adhered to because of the use of unauthorized PCs or terminals to trigger mainframe transactions. The Help Desk may find that users in a certain group are responsible for most occurrences of unauthorized software. There may be a high occurrence of service incidents arising from poorly controlled changes, or there could be a large number of RFCs or KERs relating to particular CIs. The problem management function is responsible for identifying any problems underlying such trends and for proposing corrective action to IT services management. Where there are deficiencies in IT infrastructure management procedures, the appropriate group within IT Services should put these right and report back to IT services management.

In general, IT services management should set the future direction of configuration management in the light of these management reports, taking account of planned configuration management workload and growth. See also 5.1.4.

5.1.2 CMDB backups, archives and housekeeping

Backup copies of the CMDB should be taken regularly and securely stored. It is advisable for one copy to be stored at a remote location for use in the event of a disaster. The frequency of copying and the retention policy will be dependent on the size and volatility of the IT infrastructure and the CMDB. Certain tools may allow selective copying of CI records that are new or have been changed.

The CMDB contains information on backup copies of CIs. It will also contain historic records of CIs/CI versions that are archived and possibly also of deleted CIs/CI versions. The amount of historic information to be retained depends on its usefulness to the organization. The retention policy on historic CI records should be regularly reviewed, and changed if necessary. If the cost to the organization of retaining CI information is greater than the current or potential value, do not retain it!

Typically the CMDB should contain records only for items that are physically available or could be easily created using procedures known to, and under the control of, configuration management. For guidance on the retention of software CIs please consult the **Software Control & Distribution** and **Management of Local Processors & Terminals** modules.

When configuration management has been operating for a period of time, regular housekeeping should be carried out to ensure that redundant CI records are deleted.

5.1.3 Configuration audits

Regular configuration audits must be carried out to check that the CMDB is consistent with the actual physical state of all CIs and vice-versa.

These audits should verify that all authorized versions of CIs exist and that only authorized CIs exist and are in use in the operational environment.

The configuration audits should check in addition that change records, release records etc, have been properly authorized by change management and that implemented changes are as authorized.

If there is a high incidence of unauthorized CIs detected, the frequency of configuration audits should be increased, certainly for those parts of the IT infrastructure affected by this problem.

5.1.4 Future workload and growth

The configuration management function should prepare a plan covering say, the coming 12 months in some detail and the 12 months thereafter in outline. This plan should be regularly reviewed - at least every 6 months. The plan is concerned with the configuration management workload for the period and the resources needed to service it. Checks should be made to ensure that the staff, IT resources, and support tools, including size of CMDB, available to configuration management are likely to be adequate. Where deficiencies are envisaged, steps must be taken to obtain further resources or procure enhanced support tools.

It is likely that in general configuration management activity will grow with the passage of time. The number of CIs under control and possibly the frequency of changes affecting them will increase. Information on this growth should be available from the organization's IT service, workload and capacity plans. IT services management may also decide to implement changes in the light of management reports, efficiency/effectiveness reviews and audits of the configuration management function.

At each review point, configuration management plans for the preceding period should be compared with actual events. Any deficiencies in the planning process should be rectified to improve future planning.

In considering the future work of the configuration management group, IT services management should ensure that only required configuration management data is handled. Redundant data should be purged (see 5.1.2). The cost of keeping and capturing CI details should be compared with current and potential benefits; if the current level of detail is costing too much, do not store it!

5.1.5 Reviewing for efficiency and effectiveness

The configuration management function should be periodically reviewed by IT services management for efficiency and effectiveness. As configuration management underpins a number of other IT infrastructure management functions, such as change management, problem management, the Help Desk and service level management, it is necessary to carry out a wide-ranging assessment of the state of IT management to gauge the impact of configuration management (see 3.1.17).

An initial review should be carried out shortly (approximately 3 months) after the configuration management system is implemented. In addition to reviewing the configuration management function for efficiency and effectiveness as described below, this review should check that the implementation plans have been carried out correctly and that the system is functioning as intended. Any problems detected, including those with the planning process itself, should be traced back to source and corrected as soon as possible.

Thereafter, regular formal reviews should take place - at least every 6 months (the Configuration Manager should, however, **continually** assess the efficiency and effectiveness of the configuration management function).

The information described in section 3.1.17 should be obtained and compared during the review with that for previous periods. It will be necessary to disentangle the impact of any other factors that may have impacted upon this information. The results of these comparisons must be reported for IT services management consideration, and instigation of any necessary corrective action.

The reviews should also generate the following information (not available before configuration management is implemented):

* frequency of CMDB errors and/or IT infrastructure errors caused by incorrect application of configuration management

* extent to which the CMDB has been a constantly up-to-date, complete and accurate reflection of the actual state of the IT infrastructure

* frequency of unregistered CIs within the IT infrastructure

* number and seriousness of breaches of Service Level Agreements (SLAs) that can be attributed to faults or errors in the working of the configuration management system

* frequency and impact of faults/incidents affecting the configuration management system

* frequency of occurrences when a software version in use at a remote location is incorrect because of poor configuration management/distribution/implementation

* frequency and extent of bottle-necks or delays caused by failure to carry out configuration management procedures quickly enough

* the extent to which a CMDB interrogation service, if applicable, is consistently available to allow trend analysis by appropriate IT services staff

* the extent to which regular and accurate management reports are produced

* the effectiveness of plans to cope with changes in configuration management workload and with growth in the use of configuration management (see 5.1.4).

All this information should be compared with that for the previous review periods and corrective action should be instigated, within the configuration management function or elsewhere in IT services, to rectify any problems and adverse trends.

In general there should be a gradual and continuous improvement in all efficiency/effectiveness indicators - though the rate of improvement will eventually diminish.

5.1.6 Auditing for compliance

This subsection is an example check-list for those organizations that wish to audit their configuration management function (using the organizations' computer audit section, which is independent of the IT Services section), for compliance to the procedures and advice in this module. Organizations should devise their own check-lists based on this one.

It is recommended that an audit is completed soon (eg 3 months) after the implementation of configuration management and then at least annually. Where there are particular problems in the operation of configuration management, the frequency of audits should be increased.

The following items should be examined:

* random RFCs from initiation through to implementation - are RFCs recorded in the CMDB and is change implementation controlled by configuration management?

* random CIs and RFCs affecting these CIs - is the CMDB up to date and accurate?

* are regular configuration audits carried out and are the results recorded and follow up actions performed?

* random CIs - are archived and back-up versions of CIs retained and recorded in the correct way?

* are the versions of software used in multiple locations correct?

* do CI names, version numbers etc adhere to naming conventions?

* are CI variants created and handled in accordance with laid down procedures?

* do configuration management baselines correspond to approved types of item, such as actual packages, releases, purchasable item/types - can configuration management baselines be easily and accurately created and used?

* do the contents of the DSL and the CMDB match?

* is CMDB housekeeping carried out in accordance with defined procedures?

* are reviews/forward plans carried out regularly and followed up?

* are regular and accurate reports produced for management?

* are staff adequately trained and are training records up-to-date?

The results of these audits should be included in the management reports described in 5.1.1 and followed up to ensure any deficiencies in laid down procedures or in adherence to them are corrected.

5.2 Dependencies

In addition to the dependencies listed in 3.2, audit interrogation facilities are required to check that the CMDB and the physical state of CIs are consistent (eg match record utilities for software comparison).

5.3 People

Staff recruitment, retention and training must be continued. Career advancement moves by configuration management staff to other areas within IT Services should be encouraged, provided adequate skills are retained in the Configuration Management Group. Such moves help to permeate configuration management disciplines throughout the organization and demonstrate a career path which should ease recruitment of future staff.

5.4 Timing

Configuration audits should be performed shortly after implementation of the new configuration management system, before and after major changes to the IT infrastructure, following recovery from disasters and after 'return to normal' (should be included in contingency plans), at random intervals, and in response to the detection of any unauthorized CIs.

IT services management should formally review the operation of the configuration management function and its efficiency and effectiveness shortly after implementation of the new procedures and at regular intervals thereafter, at least every six months. The management reports described in 5.1.1 should be produced for these reviews. The Configuration Manager should, however, **continually** assess the efficiency and effectiveness of the configuration management system.

A review of the expected growth of demand for configuration management activities should be conducted every six months with a one-to-two year forward window.

It is recommended that an independent audit of the configuration management function is completed soon after implementation of the new configuration management system (eg after 3 months) and then at least annually. Where particular problems are evident the frequency of audits should be stepped up.

6. Benefits, costs and possible problems

This section outlines the benefits and costs of configuration management and points out some potential problems that should be avoided.

The costs of implementing configuration management are outweighed by improved control of assets, more efficient and cheaper provision of quality IT services, better handling of changes and problems and, because it is more difficult to make malicious changes, improved security.

It is difficult to quantify all the benefits of configuration management (see 6.1) but it is reasonable to assume, for those items which can be quantified:

* an improvement in IT staff productivity (perhaps 2% to 5% overall)

* better quality IT services resulting in, say, a 1% to 2% improvement in the productivity of the users of the services.

Assuming an expenditure on configuration management equivalent to about 2% of IT staff, plus some initial investment and recurring expenditure on support tools and hardware, the balance sheet is positive, without taking account of unquantifiable benefits.

6.1 Benefits

6.1.1 Control of IT assets

Configuration items are valuable assets in themselves; for example, if a PC was stolen it would have to be replaced. Configuration management helps IT management know what its assets are supposed to be, who is responsible for their safekeeping and whether the actual inventory matches the official one.

The real value of IT assets is generally much greater than their capital value because of the part these assets play in supporting the provision of quality IT services. The consequential loss to the organization if these services are not provided can be very great. Please see sections 6.1.2 to 6.1.5.

6.1.2 Economic provision of quality IT service

The work carried out by the Configuration Management Group is largely invisible to end users.

However, configuration management helps organizations to manage change, to handle problems and to provide user support with fewer mistakes and consequently lower rework costs. In so doing, configuration management makes it easier and cheaper to provide the quality IT services upon which organizations are becoming so dependent.

6.1.3 Ability to absorb rapid change

In most organizations a high rate of change to the IT infrastructure (including the take-on of new applications software) is the norm.

Configuration management gives organizations complete control over the versions of CIs in use and in addition makes it easier for them to assess the impact of changes and to identify CIs affected by problems.

Configuration management thus greatly assists organizations to cope with changes safely, efficiently and effectively.

6.1.4 Efficient and effective handling of problems

Inevitably all IT systems are affected by incidents and problems which adversely affect the running of organizations' businesses. As far as possible, organizations should proactively prevent incidents from occurring.

Configuration management assists organizations to identify CIs affected by incidents and problems. Configuration management also assists organizations to manage the changes necessary to rectify incidents and problems.

Finally, configuration management supports the production of information on problem trends affecting CIs and thereby assists in the proactive prevention of problems.

Configuration management thus greatly contributes to the efficient and effective handling of problems.

6.1.5 Better control of software

Configuration management helps organizations to control the implementation of software changes, coupled where appropriate with hardware changes, via 'package releases'.

Package releases are required to coordinate changes that require more than one CI to be altered at a time. Increasingly this type of control of software change is becoming the norm. Implementation of change via package releases is essential when taking on high volumes of new software and when accommodating high volumes of software changes.

A package release mechanism makes it easier to test CIs that must coexist and interwork when they go live.

Packages can be developed, tested and accepted on a central system and then distributed and installed for use in remote sites.

Configuration management provides documented control of the versions of CIs to be incorporated in packages for testing and live use. Configuration management also supports the maintenance of trusted releases which can be reverted to in case of problems. (For further information please refer to the IT Infrastructure Library **Software Control & Distribution** module).

6.1.6 Improved security

Because configuration management assists IT management to control the versions of CIs in use it makes it more difficult for these to be changed maliciously. Where the scale of IT operations permits, security can be further improved by implementing definitive versions of software, and making any changes to this definitive software, on a dedicated central machine from which the software is copied for actual use.

6.1.7 Adherence to legal obligations

Configuration management maintains lists of all items of software on an IT infrastructure. CIs that come to light, via configuration audits or calls to the help desk, that are not on this list are not authorized and may well not have been paid for. Illegitimate copies can easily be identified for erasure or destruction.

Because configuration management makes software changes visible, such changes can be used to trigger investigations by IT management into possible changes that may be needed in Data Protection Act registration status.

6.1.8 Expenditure planning

Configuration management provides a complete list of CIs. It is easy to produce from this list expected maintenance costs and licence fees; maintenance contract and licence renewal dates; CI life expiry dates; and CI replacement costs (provided this information is stored).

By providing this information configuration management contributes to IT Directorates' financial planning.

6.1.9 Contingency planning

Configuration management identifies the CIs, including version numbers, in use and archived at any time; and their physical location. Provided the CMDB is copied to a suitably secure location it facilitates the restoration of IT service in the event of a disaster, by identifying the required CIs and where they are stored.

6.2 Costs

6.2.1 Resource costs

The cost of hardware and software for configuration management depends on many factors including:

* whether the organization can utilize existing hardware instead of purchasing additional equipment

* the product chosen as the configuration management tool (for example, if a tool is based upon a particular relational database product, sites currently using that product may save on licence fees)

* the number of users who are to have access the configuration management tool (multiple-user licences can be more expensive; the licence fee may increase with the number of users required)

* whether products must be tailored to the needs of the organization.

As a guide, acquisition solely of the software licences for a configuration management tool should cost in the region of £10,000 p.a. Sites acquiring hardware, a relational database and appropriate licence, and a tailored configuration management tool can expect to incur an initial expenditure of upwards of £20,000. Most sites should not expect this initial expenditure to exceed £100,000. Recurrent expenditure, for software licences and hardware maintenance, should not exceed 20 per cent of the initial outlay - provided the configuration management workload is reasonably static. Growth in the number of users and in the required hardware capacity would result in further outlays.

6.2.2 Staff costs

For each member of the configuration management team, there are salary and accommodation costs and the costs of training in configuration management and training in the use of support tools. There may be an increase in staff costs during the initial data capture exercise.

However, do not assume that configuration management staff are an overhead! If configuration management is not performed there is likely to be a net increase in staffing requirements. Time will have to be spent in correcting things that would not have gone wrong if configuration management had been in operation, and it will take more staff to handle changes and problems.

The use of configuration management will result in a better quality service which will more than repay any overhead costs.

6.2.3 Time costs

Configuration management can introduce delays, sometimes with knock-on costs, to the implementation of changes. Please see sections 6.3.3 and 6.3.4.

6.3 Possible problems

6.3.1 Using the wrong CI level

If CIs are defined at too low a level, configuration management may become involved in unnecessarily tedious detail.

If the lowest level CIs are defined at too high a level, far bigger IT infrastructure changes than are necessary may have to be implemented (eg a whole suite of programs may have to be changed in order to alter just one of the programs in the suite).

Deciding the right level of detail is not easy. The decision should hinge on the value of the information to the organization - if CI information costs more than it is likely to be worth, do not store it! If the initial level is incorrect IT management should ensure that it is changed.

6.3.2 Manual configuration management systems

Some organizations may attempt to start out with configuration management activities implemented as a manual process, with the intention of switching to automated tools when the volume of change increases. At some point, these manual systems may get overloaded and impose unreasonable delays.

The automation of configuration management activities should be started early enough to avoid overloading the initial configuration management system. In almost all cases it will be advisable to choose an automated solution from the outset.

6.3.3 Emergency changes

The need to process emergency changes must be catered for. These changes often occur in the middle of the night, or at weekends, when configuration management staff may not be on duty.

To overcome this, consider having configuration management staff working shifts, being on-call using paging devices, or delegating responsibility for configuration management activities to suitably trained staff who will be available (eg Computer Operations or Problem Management/Support staff).

6.3.4 Over-ambitious schedules

If adequate time is not built into schedules to allow configuration management staff to carry out their duties, configuration management may be perceived as a bottleneck. When package releases and other IT infrastructure changes are being scheduled, past experience of the time taken to complete configuration management activities should be taken in to account.

Even if adequate time is available and the configuration management function operates efficiently, configuration management can still be perceived as a bottleneck (see 6.3.6). However, the benefits of configuration management far outweigh any short-term time savings; so IT management should make it clear that time must be allowed for configuration management.

6.3.5 Management acceptance of configuration management

Because configuration management is a relatively new discipline to many organizations, there may be some initial reluctance to accept that it is justified. Experience has shown, however, that the costs involved are invariably less than the costs that are incurred as a result of things going wrong. Manual methods of maintaining what is in effect configuration management information are more error prone and cost more to operate.

6.3.6 Circumvention of configuration management

Some people will try to circumvent configuration management in the interests of speed or with malicious intent. Attempts must be made to overcome this problem by making such people aware of the benefits of configuration management, but if this does not work disciplinary action should be taken.

7. Tools

This section outlines the main requirements of configuration management support tools and gives information on the availability, at the time of writing, of such tools.

Configuration management tools should support the activities described in sections 3, 4 and 5 of this module and in particular should provide the following facilities.

7.1 Configuration Management Database (CMDB)

At the centre of any configuration management tool is the need for a CMDB. This database must hold a complete record of all CIs in and associated with the IT infrastructure, and the relationships between CIs. It is therefore likely that a relational database will be most suitable.

7.2 Integrated control

Ideally, support tools should allow configuration management control to be maintained, for applications software, from the outset of systems design right through to live running. Ideally, organizations should use the same tool to control all stages of the lifecycle. If this is not possible, then the IT infrastructure configuration management tool they choose should at least allow configuration management information to be transferred from a software development configuration management system, without the need for re-keying.

7.3 Change management

By holding information on the relationships between CIs, configuration management tools facilitate the impact assessment of requests for change.

To support change management, a configuration management tool should provide automated support for the following:

* the identification of related CIs affected by a proposed change in order to assist in the assessment process

* the recording of CIs which are affected by authorized changes and how (including those changes involving package releases)

* the implementation of changes including package releases in accordance with authorization records

* the recording of CI status changes when authorized changes are implemented

* the recording of 'trusted versions' of CIs and CI packages, which can be reverted to with known consequences, for example if implemented changes fail.

As far as possible, a configuration management support tool should prevent changes from being made to an IT infrastructure - whether to change the status of a CI, to implement a new version of a CI, or to create a new CI - without valid authorization via configuration management. The authorization record should automatically 'drive' the change.

The support tool should, as far as possible, force all changes, when implemented, to be recorded on the CMDB. The status (eg. live, archive, etc) of each CI affected by a change should be updated automatically when the change is implemented. Example ways in which this automatic recording of changes could be implemented include:

* automatic updating of the CMDB when software is moved between libraries, eg from 'live' to an 'archive' library

* automatic updating of the CMDB when the hardware catalogue is changed

* automatic updating of the CMDB when a package release is distributed (including to remote locations).

7.4 Other required facilities

Other required facilities are:

* sufficient security controls to limit access on a need-to-know basis

* support for CIs of varying complexity from entire systems through package releases to single hardware items and software modules and support for hierarchic and networked relationships between CIs

* easy addition of new CIs and deletion of old CIs

* automatic validation of input data (eg are all CI names unique)

* automatic establishment of all relationships that can be automatically established, when new CIs are added

* support for CIs with different model numbers, version numbers, and copy numbers

* when any CI is the subject of an incident report/ record, problem record, known error record or request for change, automatic identification of other affected CIs

* integration of problem management data within the CMDB, or at least an interface from the configuration management system to any separate problem management databases that may exist

* automatic updating and recording of the version number of a CI if the version number of any component (child) CI is changed

* maintenance of a history of all CIs (both historic record of this version - such as installation date, records of changes, previous locations etc - and of previous versions)

* support for the management and use of CI baselines (corresponding to definitive copies, versions etc) including support for reversion to trusted versions

* ease of interrogation of the CMDB and good reporting facilities, including trend analysis (eg the ability to identify the number of RFCs affecting particular CIs)

* ease of reporting of CI inventory to facilitate configuration audits

* graphical representation of sections of the CMDB (eg the ability to show graphically, configuration or network maps of interconnected CIs, and to input information on new CIs via such maps); also to show the hierarchy of relationships between parent CIs and child CIs.

7.5 Available tools

Examples of tools that are available in 1990, which provide some of these facilities, include IBM's INFO/MAN, CA's CA/Netman, SQL Software's Product Configuration Management System (PCMS), Logsys's Configuration Management Facility(CMF), Yard Software's LIFESPAN and K3's Change & Configuration Control Environment (CCC).

8. Bibliography

Glossary of Software Engineering Terminology

- ANSI/IEEE standard 729-1983 (part of Software Engineering Standards IEEE 1987: ISBN 471-63457-3).

PRINCE Configuration Management Guide - CCTA (CCTA 1989).

Software Configuration Management - J K Buckle (Macmillan 1982).

Annex A. Glossary of terms

Abbreviations and acronyms used in this module

CCTA	Central Computing and Telecommunications Agency
CMDB	Configuration Management Database
CI	Configuration Item
DSL	Definitive Software Library
IR	Incident Record or Incident Report
IT	Information Technology
KER	Known Error Record
LAN	Local Area Network
PR	Problem Record
RFC	Request for Change
SC&D	Software Control & Distribution
SLA	Service Level Agreement
WAN	Wide Area Network

Definitions of terms used in this module

Baseline	A snapshot of the state of a CI and any component CIs, frozen at a point in time for a particular purpose.
Change Record	A record containing details of which CIs are affected by an authorized change (planned or implemented) and how.
Configuration Item(CI)	A component of an IT infrastructure - or an item, such as a request for change, associated with an IT infrastructure - which is (or is to be) under the control of configuration management. CIs may vary widely in complexity, size and type - from an entire system (including all hardware, software and documentation) to a single module or a minor hardware component.

Definitive Software Library(DSL)	A library where all quality-controlled versions of all software configuration items(CIs) are held in their definitive form.
Incident Record	A record containing details of an unexpected incident affecting or deviating from the normal operation of an IT infrastructure.
Known Error Record	A record of a condition identified by successful diagnosis of the root cause of a problem, indicating that an IT infrastructure component (a CI) is at fault.
Package Release	A package of new or changed software CIs which are released together into the test and subsequently live environment.
Problem Record	A record of a condition identified from a single significant incident or from multiple incidents exhibiting common symptoms indicative of a single error, for which the cause is unknown.
Release	A new and/or changed CI which is advanced for use at a later stage in the lifecycle (eg development to test, test to live).
Release Record	A record containing details of which CIs are affected by a release (planned or implemented) and how.
Request For Change (RFC)	A form, or screen, used to record details of a request for a change to any CI within an IT infrastructure or to procedures and items associated with the IT infrastructure.
Variant	A CI that has the same basic functionality as another CI, but is different in some small way.

Annex B. Suggested CI attributes to be recorded

It is suggested that the following attributes should be recorded in the CMDB for each CI.

CI Name	The unique name by which this type of CI is known.
Copy or Serial Number	The number that uniquely identifies the particular instances of this CI - eg what software, the copy number; for hardware, the serial number.
Category	into which CI fits (eg hardware, software, documentation etc).
Type	Description of CI type, amplifying 'category' information (eg hardware configuration, software package, hardware device, program module).
Model Number (hardware)	Model of CI (corresponding for example to supplier's model number eg FDS640 model xxx, PC/AT model yyy).
Version Number	The version number of the CI.
Location	The location of the CI, eg the library or media where the software CIs reside, the site/room where terminals are located.
Officer Responsible	The name and/or designation of the officer responsible for the CI.
Responsibility Date	Date the above officer became responsible for the CI.
Source/supplier	The source of the CI, eg developed in-house, bought in from company xxxxx etc.
Supply Date	Date CI was supplied to the organization.
Accepted Date	Date CI was accepted by the organization as satisfactorily tested.
Status(current)	The current status of the CI eg test, live use, archived.
Status(scheduled)	The next scheduled status of the CI (with the date or indication of the event that will trigger the status change).
Parent CI(s) relationships	The unique CI identifier(s) - name/copy number/model number/ of the parent(s) of this CI.
Child CI(s) & relationships	The unique CI identifier(s) of all children of this CI.

Relationships	The relationship of the CI with all CIs other than parent and children (eg this CI 'uses' another CI, this CI 'is connected to' another CI, this CI is 'resident on' another CI, this CI 'can access' another CI).
RFC Numbers	The identification number of all RFCs affecting this CI.
Change Numbers	The identification number of all change records affecting this CI.
Problem Numbers	The identification number of all problem records affecting this CI.
Incident Numbers	The identification number of all incident records affecting this CI.
Comment	A comment field to be used for textual narrative; for example, to provide a description of how this version of the CI is different from the previous version.
	For RFCs, change records, package release records, etc the names, copy numbers, model numbers and version numbers, of CIs affected by the change and how they are affected, must be recorded in the CMDB. A reversion path, and the consequences of reversion, should also be recorded.

Annex C. Job description - Configuration Manager

Main Duties

1   Agrees overall objectives with IT Services Manager and works to these.

2   Arranges recruitment and training of new staff.

3   Mounts awareness campaign to win support for new configuration management procedures.

4   Proposes and agrees scope of configuration management function, items that are to be controlled, and information that is to be recorded.

5   Proposes and agrees level at which configuration items (CIs) are to be identified.

6   Proposes and agrees CI naming and numbering conventions.

7   Establishes and implements CI registration procedures.

8   Evaluates and arranges for procurement of support tools.

9   Proposes and/or agrees interfaces with change management, problem management, computer operations, network management, SC&D and finance and administration functions.

10   Plans, publicizes and oversees implementation of new configuration management function.

11   Plans and executes population of the configuration management database (CMDB).

12   Uses or provides CMDB to facilitate impact assessment for RFCs.

13   Uses or provides CMDB to help identify the other CIs affected by a fault that is affecting a CI.

14   Creates change records, package release records to specify the effect on CIs of an authorized change.

15   Uses the CMDB to ensure implemented changes are as authorized.

16   Updates the CMDB when a change is implemented
      to record the effects on the IT infrastructure of the
      change.

17   Ensures any changes to change authorization records
      are themselves subject to change management.

18   Frequently checks that the physical IT inventory is
      consistent with the CMDB and instigates any
      necessary corrective action.

19   Ensures regular housekeeping of the CMDB -
      continually plans for growth and change.

20   Instigates any action needed to secure funds and
      enhance the IT infrastructure and staffing levels to
      cope with growth and change.

21   Continually reviews the configuration management
      function for efficiency and effectiveness.

22   Assists auditors to audit the activities of the
      configuration management team for compliance to
      laid-down procedures and ensures that any
      remaining corrective action is carried out.

23   Ensures regular production of management reports,
      indicating suggested action to deal with any current
      or foreseen shortcomings.

CCTA hopes that you find this book both useful and interesting. We will welcome your comments and suggestions for improving it.
Please use this form or a photocopy, and continue on a further sheet if needed.

From:

Name

re: 1992/CONF

Organization

Address

Telephone

COVERAGE

Does the material cover your needs?
If not, then what additional material would you like included.

CLARITY

Are there any points which are unclear?
If yes, please detail where and why.

ACCURACY

Please give details of any inaccuracies found.

If more space is required for these or other comments, please continue overleaf.

OTHER COMMENTS

Further information

Further information on the contents of this module can be obtained from:

CCTA Library
Rosebery Court
St Andrews Business Park
NORWICH
NR7 0HS

Tel. 01603 704930 (GTN 30404930)

The price of this publication has been set to make a contribution to the costs incurred by CCTA in preparing the copy.

Printed in the United Kingdom for The Stationery Office
J38060 2/98 C6 10170